What Color are Your Contacts?

171 Scriptures on the Sins God hates
ENVY AND JEALOUSY

TRECE SHEPHERD-W

Bloomington, IN

authorHOUSE™

Milton Keynes, UK

AuthorHouse™
1663 Liberty Drive,
Suite 200
Bloomington, IN 47403
www.authorhouse.com
Phone: 1-800-839-8640

AuthorHouse™ UK Ltd.
500 Avebury Boulevard
Central Milton Keynes, MK9 2BE
www.authorhouse.co.uk
Phone: 08001974150

First published by AuthorHouse 7/13/2006

ISBN: 1-4259-3633-4 (sc)

Library of Congress Control Number: 2006904484

Printed in the United States of America
Bloomington, Indiana

This book is printed on acid-free paper.

Acknowledgement

Many thanks to my children: Cassandra, Debbie, and Alicia for their unconditional love, support, editing and research. To my husband, Gene Williams for being there.

To my pastor, Dr. Hughes for his encouragement and spiritual inspiration, to my church family, especially the senior choir for the songs that inspired me, thanks to Thelma, and to each choir member, to Barbara Sanders one of my dearest friends, to my brothers, William and Michael Underwood, to my sisters; Janice

Underwood and Mildred May, to my aunts; Della Griffin and Jeanette Montgomery, to Cecelia Dixon, and to my sons Paul and Keith.

This book is dedicated to my grandchildren;
Kyle, Asia, and Amari

Table of Contents

Introduction

This is very vividly explained and tells what will happen when you practice one of the sins God hates.

And even as they did not like to retain God in their knowledge, God gave them over to a reprobate mind, to do those things which are not convenient; being filled with all unrighteousness, fornication, wickedness, covetousness, maliciousness; full of envy, murder, debate, deceit, malignity; whisperers, Backbiters, haters of God, despiteful, proud, boasters, inventors of evil things,

disobedient to parents, Without understanding, covenant breakers, without natural affection, implacable, unmerciful:
Who knowing the judgment of God, that they which commit such things are worthy of death, not only do the same, but have pleasure in them that do them. *Romans: 28-32*

First episode of this deadly sins

Cain and Abel were the first two sons of Adam and Eve. No doubt, their parents had informed them of Paradise lost. Cain was a farmer and Abel was a shepherd. They each sacrificed the products of their labor to God. The Bible mentions that Abel brought the firstborn of his flocks and the fat. It only mentions that Cain offered what he grew. Somehow, it was plain to them that God was very pleased with Abel's offering. Cain was jealous and angry and finally killed Abel.

Another one

"I was the second son begotten by my father Jacob, and my mother Leah called me Simon, because the Lord had heard her prayer. I waxed strong, and shrank from no manner of deed, and I was afraid of naught, for my heart was hard, and my liver unyielding, and my bowels without mercy. And in the days of my youth I was jealous of Joseph, for our father loved him more than all the rest of us, and I resolved to kill him. For the prince of temptation sent the spirit of jealousy to take possession of me, and it blinded me so that I did not consider Joseph to be my brother,

Envy/Jealousy is

It is considered sinful because envious people ignore their own blessings, and focus on others' status rather than their own spiritual growth.

A heart condition; James 3:14
Evil; James 3:16
Breaks the peace; James 4: 1-2
The cause of death; Genesis 4: 5-7
Attempts to kill; 1 Samuel 18:11
Hatred; 1Samuel 18: 7-9
On Paul's list; Galatians 5: 19-21
Religious Jealousy; Acts 13: 45,
Acts 14:45,
Opposition; Acts 17:5
Very immature; 1 Corinthians 3:1-3
Want of someone else's belongings; Psalms 73:3,
Jealousy in the family; Luke 15:11-29
Wanting others property; Genesis 37: 9, 11
Wanting another's position; 1 John 3:12

Wanting attention or popularity; 1 Samuel 18: 7-9
Another's job; Matthew 10:13
Is not being able to inherit the earth; Galatians 5: 24

Negative attitude of Cain

Genesis 4: 3-8
[3] And in process of time it came to pass, that Cain brought of the fruit of the ground an offering unto the LORD.

[4] And Abel, he also brought of the firstlings of his flock and of the fat thereof. And the LORD had respect unto Abel and to his offering:

[5] But unto Cain and to his offering he had not respect. And Cain was very wroth, and his countenance fell.

[6] And the LORD said unto Cain, Why art thou wroth? and why is thy countenance fallen?

[7] If thou doest well, shalt thou not be accepted? and if thou doest not well, sin lieth at the door. And unto thee shall be his desire, and thou shalt rule over him.

[8] And Cain talked with Abel his brother: and it came to pass, when they were in the field, that Cain rose up against Abel his brother, and slew him.

Genesis 13

[7] And there was a strife between the herdmen of Abram's cattle and the herdmen of Lot's cattle: and the Canaanite and the Perizzite dwelled then intheland.

[8] And Abram said unto Lot, Let there be no strife, I pray thee, between me and thee, and between my herdmen and thy herdmen; for we be brethren.

Gen.16

[4] And he went in unto Hagar, and she conceived: and when she saw that she had conceived, her mistress was despised in her eyes.

[5] And Sarai said unto Abram, My wrong be upon thee: I have given my maid into thy bosom; and when she saw that she had conceived, I was despised in her eyes: the LORD judge between me and thee.

[6] But Abram said unto Sarai, Behold, thy maid is in thy hand; do to her as it pleaseth thee. And

when Sarai dealt hardly with her, she fled from her face.

Attitude of Ishmael toward Issac

Genesis 21
[**8**] And the child grew, and was weaned: and Abraham made a great feast the same day that Isaac was weaned.

[**9**] And Sarah saw the son of Hagar the Egyptian, which she had born unto Abraham, mocking.

[**10**] Wherefore she said unto Abraham, Cast out this bondwoman and her son: for the son of this bondwoman shall not be heir with my son, even with Isaac.

Envy caused by wealth

Genesis 26

[**12**] Then Isaac sowed in that land, and received in the same year an hundredfold: and the LORD blessed him.

[**13**] And the man waxed great, and went forward, and grew until he became very great:

[**14**] For he had possession of flocks, and possessions of herds, and great store of servants: and the Philistines envied him.

[**15**] For all the wells which his father's servants had digged in the days of Abraham his father, the Philistines had stopped them, and filled them with earth.

Genesis 27

[**41**] And Esau hated Jacob because of the blessing wherewith his father blessed him: and Esau said in his heart, The days of mourning for my father are at hand; then will I slay my brother Jacob.

Genesis 31

[1] And he heard the words of Laban's sons, saying, Jacob hath taken away all that was our father's; and of that which was our father's hath he gotten all this glory.

[2] And Jacob beheld the countenance of Laban, and, behold, it was not toward him as before.

[3] And the LORD said unto Jacob, Return unto the land of

thy fathers, and to thy kindred; and I will be with thee.

[**4**] And Jacob sent and called Rachel and Leah to the field unto his flock,

[**5**] And said unto them, I see your father's countenance, that it is not toward me as before; but the God of my father hath been with me.

Example of envy and sibling jealousy

Genesis 37

[**3**] Now Israel loved Joseph more than all his children, because he was the son of his old age: and he made him a coat of many colours.

[4] And when his brethren saw that their father loved him more than all his brethren, they hated him, and could not speak peaceably unto him.

[18] And when they saw him afar off, even before he came near unto them, they conspired against him to slay him.

[19] And they said one to another, Behold, this dreamer cometh.

[20] Come now therefore, and let us slay him, and cast him into some pit, and we will say, Some evil beast hath devoured him: and we shall see what will become of his dreams.

Jealous husband

Numbers 5
[12] Speak unto the children of Israel, and say unto them, If any man's wife go aside, and commit a trespass against him,
[13] And a man lie with her carnally, and it be hid from the eyes of her husband, and be kept close, and she be defiled, and there be no witness against her, neither she be taken with the manner;

[14] And the spirit of jealousy comes upon him, and he be jealous of his wife, and she be defiled: or if the spirit of jealousy come upon him, and he be jealous of his wife, and she be not defiled:

[15] Then shall the man bring his wife unto the priest, and he shall bring her offering for her, the tenth part of an ephah of barley meal; he shall pour no oil upon it, nor put frankincense thereon; for it is an offering of jealousy, an offering of memorial, bringing iniquity to remembrance.

[16] And the priest shall bring her near, and set her before the LORD:

[17] And the priest shall take holy water in an earthen vessel; and of the dust that is in the floor of the tabernacle the priest shall take, and put it into the water:

[18] And the priest shall set the woman before the LORD, and uncover the woman's head, and put the offering of memorial in her hands, which is the jealousy offering: and the priest shall have in his hand the bitter water that causeth the curse:

[**19**] And the priest shall charge her by an oath, and say unto the woman, If no man have lain with thee, and if thou hast not gone aside to uncleanness with another instead of thy husband, be thou free from this bitter water that causeth the curse:

[**20**] But if thou hast gone aside to another instead of thy husband, and if thou be defiled, and some man have lain with thee beside thine husband:

[**21**] Then the priest shall charge the woman with an oath of cursing, and the priest shall say unto the woman,

people, when the LORD doth make thy thigh to rot, and thy belly to swell;

[**22**] And this water that causeth the curse shall go into thy bowels, to make thy belly to swell, and thy thigh to rot: And the woman shall say, Amen, amen.

[**23**] And the priest shall write these curses in a book, and he shall blot them out with the bitter water:

[**24**] And he shall cause the woman to drink the bitter water that causeth the curse: and the water that causeth the curse shall enter into her, and become bitter.

[**25**] Then the priest shall take the jealousy offering out of the wom-

an's hand, and shall wave the offering before the LORD, and offer
it upon the altar:

[**26**] And the priest shall take an
handful of the offering, even the
memorial thereof, and burn it
upon the altar, and afterward
shall cause the woman to drink
the water.

[**27**] And when he hath made
her to drink the water, then it
shall come to pass, that, if she
be defiled, and have done trespass against her husband, that
the water that causeth the curse
shall enter into her, and become
bitter, and her belly shall swell,
and her thigh shall rot: and the
woman shall be a curse among
her people.

[28] And if the woman be not defiled, but be clean; then she shall
be free, and shall conceive seed.

[29] This is the law of jealousies,
when a wife goeth aside to another instead of her husband,
and is defiled;

[30] Or when the spirit of jealousy cometh upon him, and he
be jealous over his wife, and shall
set the woman before the LORD,
and the priest shall execute upon
her all this law.

[31] Then shall the man be guilt-
less from iniquity, and this woman
shall bear her iniquity.

Jealousy of Miriam and Aaron

Numbers 12

1] And Miriam and Aaron spake against Moses because of the Ethiopian woman whom he had married: for he had married an Ethiopian woman.

[2] And they said, Hath the LORD indeed spoken only by Moses? hath he not spoken also by us? And the LORD heard it.

[3] (Now the man Moses was very meek, above all the men which were upon the face of the earth.)

[4] And the LORD spake suddenly unto Moses, and unto Aaron, and unto Miriam, Come out ye three unto the tabernacle of the congregation. And they three came out.

[5] And the LORD came down in the pillar of the cloud, and stood in the door of the tabernacle, and called Aaron and Miriam: and they both came forth.

[6] And he said, Hear now my words: If there be a prophet among you, I the LORD will make myself known unto him in a vision, and will speak unto him in a dream.

[7] My servant Moses is not so, who is faithful in all mine house.

[8] With him will I speak mouth to mouth, even apparently, and not in dark speeches; and the similitude of the LORD shall he behold: wherefore then were ye not afraid to speak against my servant Moses?

[**9**] And the anger of the LORD was kindled against them; and he departed.

Deuteronomy 4

[**2**] Ye shall not add unto the word which I command you, neither shall ye diminish ought from it, that ye may keep the commandments of the LORD your God which I command you.

[**3**] Your eyes have seen what the LORD did because of Baal-peor: for all the men that followed Baal-peor, the LORD thy God hath destroyed them from among you.

[**4**] But ye that did cleave unto the LORD your God are alive every one of you this day.

Competition

1Samuel 17
[8] And Saul was very wroth, and the saying displeased him; and he said, They have ascribed unto David ten thousands, and to me they have ascribed but thousands: and what can he have more but the kingdom?

[9] And Saul eyed David from that day and forward.

[10] And it came to pass on the morrow, that the evil spirit from God came upon Saul, and he prophesied in the midst of the house: and David played with his hand, as at other times: and there was a javelin in Saul's hand.

[11] And Saul cast the javelin; for he said, I will smite David even

to the wall with it. And David avoided out of his presence twice.

[**12**] And Saul was afraid of David, because the LORD was with him, and was departed from Saul.

Jealousy in marriage

1Chronicles 15

[**28**] Thus all Israel brought up the ark of the covenant of the LORD with shouting, and with sound of the cornet, and with trumpets, and with cymbals, making a noise with psalteries and harps.

[**29**] And it came to pass, as the ark of the covenant of the LORD came to the city of David, that Michal the daughter of Saul looking out at a window saw king David dancing and playing: and she despised him in her heart.

Jealousy is death

Job 5
2] For wrath killeth the foolish man, and envy slayeth the silly one.

Jealousy of prosperity

Psalms 73
[3] For I was envious at the foolish, when I saw the prosperity of the wicked.

[4] For there are no bands in their death: but their strength is firm.

[5] They are not in trouble as other men; neither are they plagued like other men.

[6] Therefore pride compasseth them about as a chain; violence covereth them as a garment.

[7] Their eyes stand out with fatness: they have more than heart could wish.

[8] They are corrupt, and speak wickedly concerning oppression: they speak loftily.

[9] They set their mouth against the heavens, and their tongue walketh through the earth.

[10] Therefore his people return hither: and waters of a full cup are wrung out to them.

[11] And they say, How doth God know? and is there knowledge in the most High?

[12] Behold, these are the ungodly, who prosper in the world; they increase in riches.

Jealous Husband

Proverbs 6
34] For jealousy is the rage of a man: therefore he will not spare in the day of vengeance.

[35] He will not regard any ransom; neither will he rest con-tent, though thou givest many gifts.

Jealousy is cancer

[Proverbs 13
30] A sound heart is the life of the flesh: but envy the rottenness of the bones.

Proverbs 23
[16] Yea, my reins shall rejoice, when thy lips speak right things.

**[17] Let not thine heart envy sinners: but be thou in the fear of the LORD all the day long.
[18] For surely there is an end; and thine expectation shall not be cut off.**

Jealousy crueler than anger

Proverbs 27
4] Wrath is cruel, and anger is outrageous; but who is able to stand before envy?

Envy of neighbors

Ecclesiastes 4
4] Again, I considered all travail, and every right work, that for this a man is envied of his neighbour. This is also vanity and vexation of spirit.

[**5**] The fool foldeth his hands together, and eateth his own flesh.

[**6**] Better is an handful with quietness, than both the hands full with travail and vexation of spirit.

Ezekiel 8
5] Then said he unto me, Son of man, lift up thine eyes now the way toward the north. So I lifted up mine eyes the way toward the north, and behold northward at the gate of the altar this image of jealousy in the entry.

Ezekiel 16
42] So will I make my fury toward thee to rest, and my jealousy shall depart from thee, and I will be quiet, and will be no more angry.

Jealousy of vineyard workers

Matthew 20

[1] For the kingdom of heaven is like unto a man that is an householder, which went out early in the morning to hire labourers into his vineyard.

[2] And when he had agreed with the labourers for a penny a day,sent them into his vineyard.

[3] And he went out about the third hour, and saw others standing idle in the marketplace,
[4] And said unto them; Go ye also into the vineyard, and whatsoever is right I will give you. And they went their way.
[5] Again he went out about the sixth and ninth hour, and did likewise.

[**6**] And about the eleventh hour
he went out, and found others
standing idle, and saith unto
them, Why stand ye here all the
day idle?

[**7**] They say unto him, Because
no man hath hired us. He saith
unto them, Go ye also into the
vineyard; and whatsoever is right,
that shall ye receive.

[**8**] So when even was come, the
lord of the vineyard saith unto his
steward, Call the labourers, and
give them their hire, beginning
from the last unto the first.

[**9**] And when they came that
were hired about the eleventh
hour, they received every man a
penny.

[**10**] But when the first came, they
supposed that they should have

received more; and they likewise received every man a penny.

[11] And when they had received it, they murmured against the goodman of the house,

[12] Saying, These last have wrought but one hour, and thou hast made them equal unto us, which have borne the burden and heat of the day.

[13] But he answered one of them, and said, Friend, I do thee no wrong: didst not thou agree with me for a penny?
[14] Take that thine is, and go thy way: I will give unto this last, even as unto thee.

[15] Is it not lawful for me to do what I will with mine own? Is thine eye evil, because I am good?

[**16**] So the last shall be first, and the first last: for many be called, but few chosen.

Matthew 25

14] For the kingdom of heaven is as a man travelling into a far country, who called his own servants, and delivered unto them his goods.

[**15**] And unto one he gave five talents, to another two, and to another one; to every man according to his several ability; and straightway took his journey.

[**16**] Then he that had received the five talents went and traded with the same, and made them other five talents.

[**17**] And likewise he that had received two, he also gained other two.

[**18**] But he that had received one went and digged in the earth, and hid his lord's money.

[**19**] After a long time the lord of those servants cometh, and reckoneth with them.

[**20**] And so he that had received five talents came and brought other five talents, saying, Lord, thou deliveredst unto me five talents: behold, I have gained beside them five talents more.

[**21**] His lord said unto him, Well done, thou good and faithful servant: thou hast been faithful over a few things, I will make thee ruler

over many things: enter thou into the joy of thy lord.

[**22**] He also that had received two talents came and said, Lord, thou deliveredst unto me two talents: behold, I have gained two other talents beside them.

[**23**] His lord said unto him, Well done, good and faithful servant; thou hast been faithful over a few things, I will make thee ruler over many things: enter thou into the joy of thy lord.

[**24**] Then he which had received the one talent came and said, Lord, I knew thee that thou art an hard man, reaping where thou hast not sown, and gathering where thou hast not strawed:

Family jealousy

Luke 15

[**11**] And he said, A certain man had two sons:

[**12**] And the younger of them said to his father, Father, give me the portion of goods that falleth to me. And he divided unto them his living.

[**13**] And not many days after the younger son gathered all together, and took his journey into a far country, and there wasted his substance with riotous living.

[**14**] And when he had spent all, there arose a mighty famine in that land; and he began to be in want.

[15] And he went and joined himself to a citizen of that country; and he sent him into his fields to feed swine.

[16] And he would fain have filled his belly with the husks that the swine did eat: and no man gave unto him.

[17] And when he came to himself, he said, How many hired servants of my father's have bread enough and to spare, and I perish with hunger!

[18] I will arise and go to my father, and will say unto him, Father, I have sinned against heaven, and before thee,

[19] And am no more worthy to be called thy son: make me as one of thy hired servants.

[**20**] And he arose, and came to his father. But when he was yet a great way off, his father saw him, and had compassion, and ran, and fell on his neck, and kissed him.

[**21**] And the son said unto him, Father, I have sinned against heaven, and in thy sight, and am no more worthy to be called thy son.

[**22**] But the father said to his servants, Bring forth the best robe, and put it on him; and put a ring on his hand, and shoes on his feet:

[**23**] And bring hither the fatted calf, and kill it; and let us eat, and be merry:

[**24**] For this my son was dead, and is alive again; he was lost, and is found. And they began to be merry.

[**25**] Now his elder son was in the field: and as he came and drew nigh to the house, he heard musick and dancing.

[**26**] And he called one of the servants, and asked what these things meant.

[**27**] And he said unto him, Thy brother is come; and thy father hath killed the fatted calf, because he hath received him safe and sound.

[**28**] And he was angry, and would not go in: therefore came his father out, and entreated him.

[**29**] And he answering said to his father, Lo, these many years do I serve thee, neither transgressed I at any time thy commandment: and yet thou never gavest me a kid, that I might make merry with my friends:

[**30**] But as soon as this thy son was come, which hath devoured thy living with harlots, thou hast killed for him the fatted calf.

[**31**] And he said unto him, Son, thou art ever with me, and all that I have is thine.

[**32**] It was meet that we should make merry, and be glad: for this thy brother was dead, and is alive again; and was lost, and is found.

James 3

14] But if ye have bitter envying and strife in your hearts, glory not, and lie not against the truth.

16] For where envying and strife is, there is confusion and every evil work.

Jas.4

[1] From whence come wars and fightings among you? come they not hence, even of your lusts that war in your members?

[2] Ye lust, and have not: ye kill, and desire to have, and cannot obtain: ye fight and war, yet ye have not, because ye ask not.

[3] Ye ask, and receive not, because ye ask amiss, that ye may consume it upon your lusts.

Religious jealousy

Acts 13
42] And when the Jews were gone out of the synagogue, the Gentiles besought that these words might be preached to them the next sabbath.

[43] Now when the congregation was broken up, many of the Jews and religious proselytes followed Paul and Barnabas: who, speaking to them, persuaded them to continue in the grace of God.

[44] And the next sabbath day came almost the whole city together to hear the word of God.

[45] But when the Jews saw the multitudes, they were filled with envy, and spake against those things which were spoken by

Paul, contradicting and blas-
pheming.

Opposition

Acts 17

[**5**] But the Jews which believed
not, moved with envy, took unto
them certain lewd fellows of the
baser sort, and gathered a com-
pany, and set all the city on an
uproar, and assaulted the house
of Jason, and sought to bring
them out to the people.

[**6**] And when they found them
not, they drew Jason and certain brethren unto the rulers of
the city, crying, These that have
turned the world upside down
are come hither also;

1Corinthians 3

[1] And I, brethren, could not speak unto you as unto spiritual, but as unto carnal, even as unto babes in Christ.

[2] I have fed you with milk, and not with meat: for hitherto ye were not able to bear it, neither yet now are ye able.

[3] For ye are yet carnal: for whereas there is among you en-vying, and strife, and divisions, are ye not carnal, and walk as men?

2 Corinthians 12

[19] Again, think ye that we excuse ourselves unto you? we speak before God in Christ: but we do all things, dearly beloved, for your edifying.

[20] For I fear, lest, when I come, I shall not find you such as I would, and that I shall be found unto you such as ye would not: lest there be debates, envyings, wraths, strifes, backbitings, whisperings, swellings, tumults:

Breeder of envy

Galatians 5

19] Now the works of the flesh are manifest, which are these; Adultery, fornication, uncleanness, lasciviousness,

[20] Idolatry, witchcraft, hatred, variance, emulations, wrath, strife, seditions, heresies,
[21] Envyings, murders, drunkenness, revellings, and such like: of the which I tell you before, as I have also told you in time past, that they which do such things

shall not inherit the kingdom of God.

[**25**] If we live in the Spirit, let us also walk in the Spirit.

[**26**] Let us not be desirous of vain glory, provoking one another, envying one another.

Tit.3
3] For we ourselves also were sometimes foolish, disobedient, deceived, serving divers lusts and pleasures, living in malice and envy, hateful, and hating one another.

Don't compare to others

Gal.6
3] For if a man think himself to be something, when he is nothing, he deceiveth himself.

[**4**] But let every man prove his own work, and then shall he have rejoicing in himself alone, and not in another.

[**5**] For every man shall bear his own burden.

Jealousy is cruel

Songs of Solomon 8
[**6**] Set me as a seal upon thine heart, as a seal upon thine arm: for love is strong as death; jealousy is cruel as the grave: the coals thereof are coals of fire, which hath a most vehement flame.

21 Scriptures for sickness

Psalms 6
[2] Have mercy upon me, O LORD; for I am weak: O LORD, heal me; for my bones are vexed.

Psalms 103
2] Bless the LORD, O my soul, and forget not all his benefits:

[3] Who forgiveth all thine iniquities; who healeth all thy diseases;

Psalms 107
[20] He sent his word, and healed them, and delivered them from their destructions.

Prov.3
[6] In all thy ways acknowledge him, and he shall direct thy paths.

[7] Be not wise in thine own eyes: fear the LORD, and depart from evil.

[8] It shall be health to thy navel, and marrow to thy bones.

Prov.4
[20] My son, attend to my words; incline thine ear unto my sayings.

[21] Let them not depart from thine eyes; keep them in the midst of thine heart.

[22] For they are life unto those that find them, and health to all their flesh.

Proverbs 16

24] Pleasant words are as an honeycomb, sweet to the soul, and health to the bones.

Proverbs 17

[**22**] A merry heart doeth good like a medicine: but a broken spirit drieth the bones.

Isaiah 40

[**29**] He giveth power to the faint; and to them that have no might he increaseth strength.

[**30**] Even the youths shall faint and be weary, and the young men shall utterly fall:

[**31**] But they that wait upon the LORD shall renew their strength; they shall mount up with wings as eagles; they shall run, and not be

weary; and they shall walk, and not faint.

Isaiah 53
5] But he was wounded for our transgressions, he was bruised for our iniquities: the chastisement of our peace was upon him; and with his stripes we are healed.

Isaiah 58
[**8**] Then shall thy light break forth as the morning, and thine health shall spring forth speedily: and thy righteousness shall go before thee; the glory of the LORD shall be thy rereward.

Jeremiah 17
[**14**] Heal me, O LORD, and I shall be healed; save me, and I shall be saved: for thou art my praise.

Matthew 4

[**23**] And Jesus went about all Galilee, teaching in their synagogues, and preaching the gospel of the kingdom, and healing all manner of sickness and all manner of disease among the people.

Mark.6

56] And whither so ever he entered, into villages, or cities, or country, they laid the sick in the streets, and besought him that they might touch if it were but the border of his garment: and as many as touched him were made whole.

Luke 4

38] And he arose out of the synagogue, and entered into Simon's house. And Simon's wife's mother was taken with a great fever; and they besought him for her.

[**39**] And he stood over her, and rebuked the fever; and it left her: and immediately she arose and ministered unto them.

[**40**] Now when the sun was set-ting, all they that had any sick with divers diseases brought them unto him; and he laid his hands on every one of them, and healed them.

Acts 10
38] How God anointed Jesus of Nazareth with the Holy Ghost and with power: who went about doing good, and healing all that were oppressed of the devil; for God was with him.

Philippians 4

5] Let your moderation be known unto all men. The Lord is at hand.

[6] Be careful for nothing; but in every thing by prayer and supplication with thanksgiving let your requests be made known unto God.

[7] And the peace of God, which passeth all understanding, shall keep your hearts and minds through Christ Jesus.

3 John 1

2] Beloved, I wish above all things that thou mayest prosper and be in health, even as thy soul prospereth.

Emergency Numbers

When in sorrow

Call John 14

When you have sinned

Call Psalms 51

When you worry

Call Matthew 6: 19-34

When you are in danger

Call Psalms 91

When your faith needs stirring

Call Hebrews 1:1

When you feel down and out

Call Romans 8:31

When you want peace and rest
        Call Matthew 11:25-30

When the world seems bigger than GOD
        Call Psalms 90

When your purse is empty
        Call Psalms 37

When you are lonely and fearful
        Call Psalms 23

When you grow bitter and critical
        Call 1 Corinthians 13

When you need to know how to get along with your fellowman
        Call Romans 12

When you are depressed
        Call Psalms 27

When people seem Unkind
Call John 15

For eternal life and salvation
Call on the LORD

The Cancer

Jealousy can become like a cancer. It can start out very small and escalate into a consuming evil that eats away at your very soul. I believe jealousy occurs when some one has something that you want and you think it is not attainable for you.
Jealousy breeds negativity. You may hear something like, "They think that _____ because they got _____ (you fill in the blanks) It is most often a statement that is made to satisfy the quilt a person may carry for not doing their best to reach a similar goal.

Beware of the statement, "God will take it away." God is not going to take the blessing from you because a jealous hearted person says so or because you don't share with everyone. You don't need to justify to your friends or others as to why you received the blessing. You only need to thank and praise God. Blessings are defaulted by lack of responsibility to keep it or for not being thankful for the blessing. *And we know that all things work together for the good to them that love God*
Romans 8:28

A Reflection

I am a reflection of many challenges and struggles faced by many of you. Some are the same events and some are similar situations. No one goes unsuffered. We all suffer at some point. There is no road that extends long enough that doesn't get a turn. There is no lifetime that lives long enough that doesn't get a turn. There are potholes all around us. Sometimes we fall into one. Just remember where it is and try not to fall into it again. We must learn from our mistakes. There are many more potholes out there to fall into. Some have even been placed there for you to fall into... watch out!

Stop the jealousy...
you can do it too!

Don't apologize for the blessings God has given you unless you are unhappy with them. Don't let anyone make you feel guilty for your accomplishments and achievements. Heaven is full of blessings all anyone has to do is ask? Some of us try to make others feel guilty for having a formal education, a car of your choice, a house to your liking, and clothes that you choose to purchase. Lets briefly address each on of them.
Your degree is something that most of us sacrificed in various ways to earn. I sacrificed time

spent with my family so that I could make a better life for them. I worked two jobs and went to college evenings. There were times I did not see my children during a 24-hour period. If it was not for my oldest daughter Cassandra, I would not have been able to accomplish this goal. I give God the glory, and her all the credit. My baby girl once told me she thought Cassandra was her mother. That was very painful for me to hear.

The audacity, the gall, the nerve for someone to make the statement, "she thinks she is something because she got that little ole degree" is.

You are correct! Yes that was something that I am proud of. Yes... I do think I am something! I did it at a cost!

You can do it too!

Most often you buy the car of your choice. When you are shopping for a car you usually have one or two people in mind, yourself or your family members. Since you are going to have to pay for the car with money you worked for, you usually choose what you like and can afford. Next in mind is your family if there are children. Who are you to say, "Why did he/she get that expensive car?" Choice is the answer.

You can do it too!

The house you have saved for and went without some of the pleasures of life to save for that down payment. You like the house with three bedrooms and three baths on the corner. God has blessed you with the right amount of money for the down payment at the right time the house becomes for sale. Your credit score may not be 750, but God is in the plan and you get approved. You finally close and prepare to move in. What a feeling! Do you think you need to apologize for this awesome blessing? I don't think so.

You can do it too!

Your clothes and what you pay for them is the image you want to portray. The image that makes you feel good about yourself; the image that can make you happy, the cost is personal. Quality costs, **and you can do it too!** Delight thyself also in the Lord; and he shall give thee the desires of thine heart. Commit thy way

unto thee Lord; trust also in him;
and he shall bring it to pass.
  Psalm 37: 4 and,5

The "Fixum" Mentality!

If I make an error according to **your** measuring stick, then don't "fix" me pray for me. Somewhere, somehow some folks have the notion that they are suppose to punish by a series of fixes. To name a few: if you don't agree with them on any and every-thing, if you don't heed to their advice, if you don't loan when you are asked, if you don't invite when they think you should, then there is a very good chance that you are going to be fixed. You may never get spoken to again. You will be a target of gossip; you may get dreadful things wished upon you. This behavior could continue for years until you become a victim of sorts and then these words maybe spoken, "I told you something would happen. He/she had to ask me for help."

It is the Lord's mercies that we are not consumed, because his compassions fail not. They are new every morning: great is thy faithfulness.

Lamentations 3:22 and 23

I have a friend whose name I will not disclose. She is one of the most caring persons one could ever meet. She helps everyone that expresses a need and helps some that doesn't express a need. No doubt she may have made some mistakes in her lifetime that she is probably not proud of and that applies to all of us.

(We are all EX something!) But some want to place their measuring stick on her and say, 'She should not have done that." Well take a look at the long list of things we have done in our lives, and say I should not have done that. Don't use your measuring stick on her. Let live and let GOD! Her salvation comes from God... not you! Her prayer and my prayer are, "God I repent of my sins, I open my heart and accept you as my Lord and savior."

Jealousy Quotes

Want to know who your true friends are? Pretend like you are sick or pretend to be broke.

> Trece Shepherd-W

Disappointment lies in expectation. TSW

Guilt can breed jealousy TSW

It is not the size of the gift. The gift is knowing that you are important or special enough for someone to give a gift. Is that not what GOD did? TSW

My Glossary

(You want find these in Webster. I have formed the definitions based on my experiences.)

Enviology
Enviology, n. a practitioner of envious and jealous behavior and or activities.

Offensive Jealousy, n. causing anger, an attack on a person receving recognition for an accomplishment, achievement, an ability, a gift, a possession. To cause a pesron to be resented or cause an action of attack. pretending to help advance a person's dreams or goals to only find out your plans to either run with it themselves or pass the information to someone else.

Defensive Jealousy, n. intended to deter or prevent another from getting points on an achievement or an accomplishment. An attitude that is perceived to threaten their ego. Outright tackle on what ever you try to achieve. An attempt to block your accomplishments from being known; turn a conversation to keep from talking or congratulating a person.

Silent Jealousy, n. don't mention the achievement, talk about everything else. Pretend that they were not aware of it.

Green-hearted, adj. A person with seemingly good intentions, which is contaminated with envy. **Measuring stick,** n. Your set of standards used on another.

Dictionary definitions

Envy n 1: a feeling of grudging admiration and desire to have something possessed by another [syn: <u>enviousness</u>, <u>the green-eyed monster</u>] 2: spite and resentment at seeing the success of another (personified as one of the deadly sins) [syn: <u>invidia</u>] v 1: feel envious towards; admire enviously 2: be envious of; set one's heart on [syn: <u>begrudge</u>]A feeling of discontent and resentment aroused by and in conjunction with desire for the possessions or qualities of another. the desire for another's traits, status, abilities, station, or worldly goods. It need not be associated with an object; its salient characteristic is the unfavorable comparison of one's own status with that of another.

Jealousy a feeling of jealous envy (especially of a rival) [syn: **green-eyed monster] is an emotion experienced by one who perceives that another person is giving something that s/he wants or feels is due to them**

the green-eyed monster
n : a feeling of grudging admiration and desire to have something possessed by another [syn: envy, enviousness]

A Drop of Sunshine

Let us not be so arrogant in our own way of doing things that we fail to see others way of doing a thing. Don't fail to take the opportunity to sunshine in someone else's accomplishments. Congratulate when it is in order. Praise the person's efforts when it is in order. Smile at a face, any face. There is no human that doesn't like praise and acknowledgement of their efforts. God gave us all the ability to be a drop of sunshine to help change other's lives. To give a drop of sunshine is free. The cost is nothing but a caring moment.

Trece Shepherd-W

It is considered sinful because envious people ignore their own blessings, and focus on others' status rather than focusing on their own spiritual growth.

A Prayer for the Jealousy Hearted
by Trece Shepherd -W

Heavenly father I come to you as
humble as I know how to be.
I give you all the glory, the honor,
and the praise.
I ask you oh Lord to remove from
my heart the ill will and bad feeling that I have for

_____
(Person's name)
Help me oh lord to remove this
pain that makes me hurt inside
when someone else is called
upon, praised or chosen over me.
Please God help me see the gifts
that you have given me and that
I may be able to use them in the

way that you would have me. Let
your will be done oh God!
Oh Lord set me free from the
envy that weighs my soul, re-
lease me from the art of decep-
tion to hurt others, give me the
self-control
I ask in your son Jesus name
Amen!

The Story of the Envious Man and of Him Who Was Envied

In a town of moderate size, two men lived in neighbouring houses; but they had not been there very long before one man took such a hatred of the other, and envied him so bitterly, that the poor man determined to find another home, hoping that when they no longer met every day his enemy would forget all about him. So he sold his house and the little furniture it contained, and moved into the capital of the country, which was luckily at no great distance. About half a mile from this city he bought a nice little place, with a large garden and a fair-sized court, in the centre of which stood an old well.

In order to live a quieter life, the good man put on the robe of a dervish, and divided his house into a quantity of small cells, where he soon established a number of other dervishes. The fame of his virtue gradually spread abroad, and many people, including several of the highest quality, came to visit him and ask his prayers.

Of course it was not long before his reputation reached the ears of the man who envied him, and this wicked wretch resolved never to rest till he had in some way worked ill to the dervish whom he hated. So he left his house and his business to look after themselves, and betook himself to the new dervish monastery, where he was welcomed by the founder with all the warmth imaginable. The excuse he gave for his appearance was that he had come to consult the chief of the dervishes on a private matter of great importance. "What I have to say must not be overheard," he whispered; "command, I beg of you, that your dervishes retire into their cells, as night is approaching, and meet me in the court."

The dervish did as he was asked without delay, and directly they were alone together the envious man began to tell a long story, edging, as they walked to and fro, always nearer to the well, and when they were quite close, he seized the dervish and dropped him in. He then ran off triumphantly, without having been seen by anyone, and congratulating himself that the object of his hatred was dead, and would trouble him no more.

But in this he was mistaken! The old well had long been inhabited (unknown to mere human beings) by a set of fairies and genii, who caught the dervish as he fell, so that he received no hurt. The dervish himself could see nothing, but he took for granted that something strange had happened, or he must certainly have been dashed against the side of the well and been killed. He lay quite still, and in a moment he heard a voice saying, "Can you guess whom this man is that we have saved from death?"

"No," replied several other voices.

And the first speaker answered, "I will tell you. This man, from pure goodness of heart, forsook the town where he lived and came to dwell here, in the hope of curing one of his neighbours of the envy he felt towards him. But his character soon won him the esteem of all, and the envious man's hatred grew, till he came here with the deliberate intention of causing his death. And this he would have done, without our help, the very day before the Sultan has arranged to visit this holy dervish, and to entreat his prayers for the princess, his daughter."

"But what is the matter with the princess that she needs the dervish's prayers?" asked another voice.

"She has fallen into the power of the genius Maimoum, the son of Dimdim," replied the first voice. "But it would be quite simple for this holy chief of the dervishes to cure her if he only knew! In his convent there is a black cat which has a tiny white tip to its tail. Now to cure the princess the dervish must pull out seven of these white hairs, burn three, and with their smoke perfume the head of the princess. This will deliver her so completely that Maimoum, the son of Dimdim, will never dare to approach her again."

The fairies and genii ceased talking, but the dervish did not forget a word of all they had said; and when morning came he perceived a place in the side of the well which was broken, and where he could easily climb out.

The dervishes, who could not imagine what had become of him, were enchanted at his reappearance. He told them of the attempt on his life made by his guest of the previous day, and then retired into his cell. He was soon joined here by the black cat of which the voice had spoken, who came as usual to say good-morning to his master. He took him on his knee and seized the opportunity to pull seven white hairs out of his tail, and put them on one side till they were needed.

The sun had not long risen before the Sultan, who was anxious to leave nothing undone that might deliver the princess, arrived with a large suite at the gate of the monastery, and was received by the dervishes with profound respect. The Sultan lost no time in declaring the object of his visit, and leading the chief of the dervishes aside, he said to him, "Noble scheik, you have guessed perhaps what I have come to ask you?"

"Yes, sire," answered the dervish; "if I am not mistaken, it is the illness of the princess which has procured me this honour."

"You are right," returned the Sultan, "and you will give me fresh life if you can by your prayers deliver my daughter from the strange malady that has taken possession of her."

"Let your highness command her to come here, and I will see what I can do."

The Sultan, full of hope, sent orders at once that the princess was to set out as soon as possible, accompanied by her usual staff of attendants. When she arrived, she was so thickly veiled that the dervish could not see her face, but he desired a brazier to be held over her head, and laid the seven hairs on the burning coals. The instant they were consumed, terrific cries were heard, but no one could tell from whom they proceeded. Only the dervish guessed that they were uttered by Maimoum the son of Dimdim, who felt the princess escaping him.

All this time she had seemed unconscious of what she was doing, but now she raised her hand to her veil and uncovered her face. "Where am I?" she said in a bewildered manner; "and how did I get here?"

The Sultan was so delighted to hear these words that he not only embraced his daughter, but kissed the hand of the dervish.

Then, turning to his attendants who stood round, he said to them, "What reward shall I give to the man who has restored me my daughter?"

They all replied with one accord that he deserved the hand of the princess.

"That is my own opinion," said he, "and from this moment I declare him to be my son-in-law."

Shortly after these events, the grand-vizir died, and his post was given to the dervish. But he did not hold it for long, for the Sultan fell a victim to an attack of illness, and as he had no sons, the soldiers and priests declared the dervish heir to the throne, to the great joy of all the people.

One day, when the dervish, who had now become Sultan, was making a royal progress with his court, he perceived the envious man standing in the crowd. He made a sign to one of his vizirs, and whispered in his ear, "Fetch me that man who is standing out there, but take great care not to frighten him." The vizir obeyed, and when the envious man was brought before the Sultan, the monarch said to him, "My friend, I am delighted to see you again." Then turning to an officer, he added, "Give him a thousand pieces of gold out of my treasury, and twenty waggon-loads of merchandise out of my private stores, and let an escort of soldiers accompany him home." He then took leave of the envious man, and went on his way.

Now when I had ended my story, I proceeded to show the genius how to apply it to himself. "O genius," I said, "you see that this Sultan was not content with merely forgiving the envious man for the attempt on his life; he heaped rewards and riches upon him."

People outside the family who have had an important role during the ins and outs of my life.

Rev. Arthur Hughes Jr.
Robert Boss
Jerry Ammons
Barbara J. Sanders
Jeanette Foster
Annetia Reed
Percy Lofton
Eloys Goon
William Townsend
Johnny Miller
Jessie Toy
Gwen Mc Ghee
Loesther Foley

About the Author

Trece Shepherd-W Received her Bachelor Of Education from Chicago State University, Chicago, Illinois, a Masters Degree In Education from National; Lewis University in Evanston, Illinois. Mother of three daughters and grandmother to two grandsons, Kyle and Amari, and one grand daughter, Asia.

This is the second book of a three part series. First book titled *101 Scriptures on One of the Sins God Hates...Gossip*

She and her husband live in Helena West Helena, Arkansas and are members of Greater

First Baptist Church; she is the first woman to be elected to the city council of the newly con-solidated city of Helena West Helena, Arkansas.